Is God Happiness?

A Book of Spiritual Contemplation, Hope and Inspiration

Michael John DeNucci

© Michael John DeNucci

No portion of this text can be copied or reproduced without the express written consent of Michael John DeNucci.

Cover photo credit: Michael John DeNucci

Michael John DeNucci
Cumberland, WI
September 2023

Second Edition Published 2023

First Edition Published 2021

Acknowledgments

I thank my siblings and friends for supporting me in writing this book. In particular, I thank my brothers Peter and Donald, my friend Kristina Young and a great special thank you goes out to my brother Tony for facilitating printing of this book.

Finally, but foremost, I thank God who, through the Holy Spirit, inspired me to write this book. My gratitude to God is overwhelming!

Preface

The purpose of this book is to bring happiness to everyone based on their relationship with God. I believe God is happiness in this lifetime and the next in that place we call heaven.

THERE IS NO DOWNSIDE TO GOD'S LOVE! IT IS UNCONDITIONAL AND RELIABLE! THAT IS THE CASE I WILL BUILD IN THIS BOOK.

Introduction

My brother Peter wrote three books about safety, being an airline pilot much of his career. In his first book entitled "Captain's Discretion" he considered the element of "distraction" leading to danger and possible accidents in the airline industry, which could be applied elsewhere. So, I extend the idea of "distraction" to worldly concerns distracting us from God. Such distraction can and does jeopardize our happiness. God is Happiness

Table of Contents

1. Is Happiness a Myth?
2. Do All Souls Live Forever?
3. The Holy Spirit
4. Awakened by the Holy Spirit
5. God's Plan
6. Love Our Neighbor as Ourselves
7. Love: Viewed as a Business Decision?
8. Forgiveness
9. Penance
10. Does Original Sin Exist?
11. My Mission in Life
12. Sincerity and Humility
13. Life Satisfaction
14. Fear and Courage
15. Suffering: Why?
16. Thanking God at Day's End
17. God Thanks Us
18. Fear and Worry
19. Intelligence or Wisdom?
20. Hope and God's Love
21. Listening to Others
22. Patience

23. Catholic Confession: Necessary for Forgiveness of Sin?
24. Indifference
25. Do We Try to Please People and Rule out Pleasing God?
26. Like God, We Can Be Love
27. Music: It's Value to Happiness
28. Invitations Rather Than Scares
29. Love and Helping Others
30. What Does God Demand of Us? Having the Courage to Do Good Deeds
31. Does God Need to Earn Our Trust?
32. Celebrating Life
33. Fear and Hatred
34. Is Fun Inherently Evil?
35. God Loves Us
36. Can We Experience Happiness without Having to Pay for it Later?
37. God is There to Help Us
38. Should We Ever Hate Ourselves for Sinning?
39. Is Morality Absolute or Relative?
40. Can God be Offended?
41. How to be Your Own Best Friend
42. Is it OK to Have a Need for Love?
43. Prayer and Politics

44. Are Humility and Self Love Related?
45. Prayer and Conscience
46. Pleasing and Trusting God
47. The Search for the Truth
48. Jesus before Pontus Pilate
49. Jesus: I am the Way, the Truth and the Life
50. Are Humility and Self Hatred Related?
51. How is God within Us?
52. If God is within Us, Does that Make us God?
53. Are Humility and Self Love Mutually Exclusive?
54. What Defines our Relationship with Others?
55. Love and Forgiveness
56. Happiness: Divine Providence
57. Using People
58. Integrity
59. Consequences of Our Actions
60. Do We Take God for Granted?
61. God's Plan for Us
62. Making Excuses for Sinning
63. What is Accomplishment?
64. Trust and Jesus
65. God the Father
66. Can We be Saints?
67. Anger and Humility
68. Is it Judgmental to Criticize Persons' Actions?

69. Jesus: Are We Just Lukewarm for Him?
70. Who was Jesus?
71. Spiritual Love
72. Non-Christian Religions
73. Resurrection of the Dead: Heaven and Hell
74. Count Our Blessings
75. Look at the Positive when Contemplating the Future
76. God Answers Our Prayers
77. What is Laziness?
78. Karma: What Goes Around Comes Around
79. Humility: Admitting when We are Wrong
80. Jesus: His Ascension into Heaven and His Second Coming
81. Health of the Soul
82. Order: The First Law of the Universe
83. Regrets: Do They have Value?
84. Humility: Self Love and Loving Other
85. God is Love: Regrets and Forgiveness
86. Fear of the Lord
87. My Testimony and Religion
88. Respect
89. God's Love and Suffering
90. Why Did Christ Die on the Cross?
91. Penance: Interior and Exterior

92. Happiness and Material Goods
93. Morning and Evening Prayer
94. Happiness from Within
95. God Help Us!
96. Has God Changed?
97. My Prayer
98. Prejudging People
99. The Value of Anticipation
100. Perfection
101. Anger and Forgiveness
102. God is Love, from which Comes Forgiveness
103. Giving the Gift Back to God
104. St. Michael the Archangel
105. Why is Trust so Difficult at Times?
106. Does God ever Apologize to Us?
107. Prayer: Should it be Work?
108. Forgiveness and Trust
109. Are We, Today, Responsible for the Passion and Death of Christ?
110. The Freedom to Love
111. Life as Going through a Maze
112. Jesus: Does He Remain in Us When We Sin?
113. What is a Companion?
114. The Old Testament
115. The New Testament

116. Does Jesus Ever Want Us to Hate Ourselves?
117. NEVER say "Go to Hell" to Anyone!
118. Patience and Anger
119. Is Law There to Serve Us or for Us to Serve It?
120. The Fruits of the Holy Spirit
121. Coming Out of Covid 19 Restrictions
122. Is Love Proper?
123. Freedom: Is it a Myth?
124. Is There a Difference between Fun and Good Times?
125. Is Money the Root of All Evil?
126. Fairness in Relationships
127. Cooperation vs. Competition
128. Trust in God and Others Can Bring Happiness
129. Is the "Devil" Responsible for Our Sins?
130. Jesus: The Mandate to Love!
131. Love: Does It Mean Never Having to Say "I am Sorry?"
132. Is it Better to Give than to Receive?
133. The Gift of Love
134. The Legacy of Jesus: Love for God and Others as Ourselves
135. Today: Opportunity for Happiness

1
Is Happiness a Myth?

When I was much younger, perhaps in the 1960s or 1970s, it was said that happiness was a myth; that we fool ourselves by thinking it is real, something we can strive for that is real. Also, the idea that God was dead was proposed at that time. To me that suggests defeat or even despair. There was no hope for Happiness—not even from a living God—according to those statements.

Happiness is not a myth and is something very real that can be attained in this lifetime, not only in that place we call Heaven after we die.

Scripture says, according to Jesus, that the Kingdom of Heaven is within us. Therefore, this "Kingdom within Us" can bring us Happiness in this lifetime on earth.

That is not to say that people cannot be sad or even depressed, but that they can experience Happiness if they persevere with love and truth, which is the foundation of all love.

To quote St. Paul in his Letter to the Corinthians: "There is no limit to Love's Forbearance, it's Truth, it's Hope, it's Power to Endure." This Love does not occur only in an exclusive relationship such as marriage. It can and should be in all human relationships.

2
Do All Souls Live Forever?

The Good News is that Jesus Christ promised "Everlasting Life" for those souls that love Him. Our earthly bodies die, but our souls will live on forever if we believe in Jesus Christ. That beginning of "Heaven" can start right here in our earthly life. Jesus said the Kingdom of Heaven is within us. This Kingdom can be "Heaven on Earth" and continue in that place we call Heaven after our earthly bodies die. "Eye has not seen, Ear has not heard, and Mind has not imagined what God has in store for those who love Him." (From the New Testament)

3
The Holy Spirit

I think that some of us do not give enough attention to the Holy Spirit. The Holy Spirit is the Advocate and the Comforter. Advocate is defined as someone who defends or argues for a specific cause. In this case it would be for truth and life which is Jesus Christ.

The Holy Spirit came to the upper room to inspire the first Apostles on Pentecost to evangelize or spread the news about the Risen Christ. The Holy Spirit spoke to them in fiery tongues so that the apostles could spread the news about Jesus in languages foreign to themselves. When the Apostles came out, the persons outside were amazed that they could speak so many languages.

Jesus also promised the Comforter, which was also the Holy Spirit. Thus, the Holy Spirit is at least Inspiration and Comfort for us.

4
Awakened by the Holy Spirit

One night I was awakened from sleep by a voice in my head like in a dream. The voice in my head said: "I am the Holy Spirit." I became very frightened. The voice said "Write down that I am the Holy Spirit". Then I fell back to sleep, but was awakened again with the same message. Then it happened again for the third time. I was worried that I was losing sleep. Finally, for a fourth time I was awakened by the message that my time had come: "This is a dream come true for you, Mike. You are doing what had been sleeping in your mind. You are writing books. Write that down." I felt bad that I had lost sleep, but then thought the message from the Holy Spirit was more important than getting a good night's sleep. So I wrote what I have told you. I realize that the message from the Holy Spirit has been true and I must thank the Holy Spirit for that inspiration.

5
God's Plan

At times it seems to me that we have no free will, but are predestined because everything that happens is God's will. God knows what we will do before we do it. But we do have free will. If we surrender to God, our plan and God's plan will come together. We must accept God completely. Then our lives will unfold as they should according to His plan, which is Happiness for us.

6
Love Our Neighbor as Ourselves

Jesus commands that we Love our Neighbor as ourselves. This gift of love should be given to others with no expectations in return from those we love. We should not expect praise or monetary return from others for our love.

But if do get reciprocation from others, that is a bonus. If we do not get that bonus from others, we have been promised our reward from Jesus: Everlasting Happiness!

(None of this is meant to say that no payment in business dealing should be expected. Fairness in business is actually required, of course.)

7
Love: A Business Decision?

Too often, I think we view love as a business decision: In accounting; will our revenue exceed our expenses to yield a profit? In finance, what will be the rate of return on our investment? As said in article 6, Jesus Christ has promised us the reward for loving others when we expect nothing in return: Heaven or Everlasting Happiness!

8
Is There Love without Forgiveness?

Is there love if someone has offended us and we do not forgive them? No, there is no love in that. Likewise, if we offend someone and ask for forgiveness and they do not forgive us, there is no love. It is best that someone asks for forgiveness in order to forgive them. But sometimes that does not happen. I believe that, in such cases, we should still forgive them, but are not obligated to continue the relationship if neither wants it.

9
Penance

Penance is defined as an action to do atonement for sin. Atonement is defined as reconciliation. Regarding atonement to God for sin, I use this example: If someone offends me, would I say to that person: if you do these favors for me, I will forgive you. If you do not do these favors, I will not forgive you. (These favors can be considered penance as atonement to me for the offense). I could not say that to that person, but that that he/she is simply forgiven with no favors to me and atonement is done.

Why would God be any less forgiving, requiring favors to Him to be forgiven? God's love is unconditional and He loves all of us.

10
Does Original Sin Exist?

My simple flat answer if NO! How can a baby born through the power of God be in a state of sin? What has that baby done to sin? How could that baby's soul be impure?

The "story" of Adam and Eve in the Bible (Genesis, possibly written by Moses) is a story and that is all. It is meant to teach a lesson, which is we could not succumb to evil until, so the story goes, Adam and Eve ate of the forbidden fruit and could then know good and evil. To me this means that man evolved from animals and knew good from evil only after God put a soul into that being and it became man, knowing good and evil. But the most important lesson of all is that IF WE

DISOBEY GOD WE WILL SUFFER. The suffering of Adam and Eve is that they had the "burden" of knowing morality and could fail God and then suffer, unlike the animals from which they evolved, who did not know morality, so could not suffer after doing wrong according to some conscious moral code. However, their sin was NOT passed down to us as original sin.

Turning to Baptism, it is an important sacrament, but not to remove original sin, which does not exist. Baptism is meant to initiate us into Christianity. It should not be done on babies, but on persons who have reached the age of reason and are ready to be initiated into Christianity. Then, the person to be baptized can understand the meaning of the process.

I watched a child of about 6 or 7 years old become baptized at a local Christian Church. The child said before being immersed in to a tank of water, "I accept Jesus Christ as my Personal Savior". This type of Baptism makes sense to me and it follows from Christ's commandment given to his apostles to "Baptize all nations in the Name of The Father, The Son and The Holy Spirit".

11
My Mission in Life

My Mission in life is to know, love and serve God. I do this with my Books and my example. If I do not do this, I would consider my life as a failure. Thus, I do not measure my success in terms of dollars and cents (money) or material success in any way. Up till now all my books have been given away as free gifts. I may continue this path for all my books. However, I must listen to the Holy Spirit to know which path—a relatively small readership through gifts—or reaching a larger audience through asking money for my books to cover real publishing and marketing costs or putting my books on the internet as E-Books. I must listen to the Holy Spirit to know God's Plan for me. Anyway, thank you for reading this book and my other books, if you have read them.

12
Sincerity and Humility

Without Sincerity there can be no Humility and without Humility there can be no Sincerity. They go hand in hand. If we do not have humility, which is seeing ourselves without false pride, we cannot have honesty concerning ourselves and others. Without sincerity, we lie to ourselves and others and our message to others is false—a lie. To be truthful to ourselves and others we must have humility and sincerity. Then, we are ready to humbly pray to God for direction in our lives. Then, we can be sincere with others to find out what we really want to do about others. I have found that my mission is to give love and not worry about getting love back. Love will conquer all!

13
Life Satisfaction

I learned about job satisfaction in my graduate school studies of Industrial Relations. However, that was a rather narrow view of satisfaction. What I propose to consider is "Life Satisfaction".

To assume every day will be the same is to put every day on a plateau with no ups or downs. But, if we are fixated on that plateau it can become a rut.

To gain satisfaction in life, we must leave that plateau or rut at times to do something creative or at least "outside the box". It is not necessary to feel uncomfortable to move "outside the box", though that could be a result. However, outside the box we may feel inspired to express ourselves in a meaningful way by harnessing our creativity. That can result in "Life Satisfaction", which can mean the beginning of Heaven before our earthly bodies die. Jesus wants us to be happy in this lifetime and the next.

14
Fear and Courage

When encountering fear, we can deal with it in various ways. First, we can give in to it without doing anything, except being fearful. This approach causes anxiety and prevents us from moving forward. The second way is that we can take steps by being cautious and avoid the object or process that we fear. Finally, if the source of the fear cannot be avoided, we can face it head on and take action to conquer it, because we do not know the outcome, but have faith that we can conquer it. Love Conquers All!

15
Suffering: Why?

Though God does not want any of us to suffer and does not enjoy watching suffering, He may allow it to help us realize our weaknesses and vulnerabilities. This allows us the humility to look to God, not just ourselves, for relief. Thus, by increasing our faith in God, we can have more hope for the suffering to end and find happiness.

16
Thanking God at Day's End

I find it easy to thank or acknowledge God upon waking up in the morning. But, too often I do not thank God for the day just ending. That "thank you" to God is important too. I must remember it and ask for God to be with me even during sleep: "Now I lay me down to sleep, pray the Lord my soul to keep, and if I die before I wake, pray the lord my souls will take".

17
God Thanks Us

Too often, I think, we do not consider that God thanks us for our good deeds and attention given to Him. Remember, God is Love, so He always thanks us because Love is not rude and it would be rude for Him not to thank us, just as it would be rude for us not to thank Him. God always loves us and rewards us for our manifestations of Love through our good deeds.

18
Fear and Worry

Jesus told us not to worry about tomorrow. Jesus said: Look at the birds and even the lilies of the field. Do not worry about what will we eat and wear. A while ago, a friend of mine was worrying that he had lost a lot of money in the stock market and feared he would lose much more. Worrying about something over which we have no control over ruins the present, and it may be over something that never happens. The Serenity Prayer say it well: God grant me the Serenity to change the things I can change and accept the things I cannot change and the Wisdom to know the difference.

Also, worrying about the past is useless and leads nowhere. What has been done cannot be undone.

It has been said: the past is history, the future is a mystery and the present is a gift. That's why they call it the present.

19
Intelligence or Wisdom?

Intelligence is the ability to gain knowledge by understanding something. However, wisdom is gained from knowledge to make sound decisions based on that knowledge. Wisdom comes from the Holy Spirit for me and guides me through my writings in my books to present Love of God, neighbor and self. Although Wisdom comes from the Holy Spirit, it uses my personal experiences as a source for my books. These experiences include reading of Scripture and religious/spiritual books or writings.

20
Hope and God's Love for Us

When we are in our darkest hours, we should remember that God Loves Us. He offers us Hope if we just pray for it. He will never forsake us and loves us always, in good times and bad. His Love is 100% reliable.

21
Listening to Others

If we listen to others and simply say "no" to everything they say and go on to what we want to say, that is NOT listening. Who are we to say what they say does not matter. We should always keep an open mind to truly listen and give their words a chance, instead of just saying what we want to say. If we do not listen it shows that we have false pride. True listening requires humility, which is a virtue and actually leads us to Happiness.

22
Patience

It has been said that "patience is a virtue" and "good things come to those who wait". St Paul said in his letter to the Corinthians "love is patient".

I have been working on the virtue of humility and believe I had made progress. However, I am not proud of that progress lest I defeat humility itself.

But, patience is something I have to go a long way on. I seem to like immediate gratification and immediate results from my efforts. To learn patience, I must surrender to God and trust that He will give me what I need in due time. God is Happiness!

23
Catholic Confession: Is It Necessary for Forgiveness of Sin?

No! What of all the Non-Catholics and even Catholics who do not go to confession after every sin. Certainly, they can be forgiven if they repent of their sins. St. Paul said : "confess your sins to one another." But this was before the formal beginning of the Catholic Church. Jesus told the Apostles that "whoever sins you forgive, they are forgiven and whoever sins you shall retain, they are retained." But, again this was before the formal start of the Catholic Church.

Thus, the dilemma . I do believe all persons should confess their sins to God. The Lord's Prayer says: "forgive us our trespasses (sins) as we forgive those who trespass (sin) against us".

The Catholic confession requires, or at least used to require, that we say as Act of Contrition as follows: "Oh my God I am heartily sorry for having offended thee because of thy just punishment, but Most of ALL because I have Offended Thee, my God, who art all good and deserving of all my love. I firmly resolve with the help of thy grace to sin no more and to avoid all near occasion of sin". This prayer seems to me like a perfect prayer for forgiveness from God. However, I believe that God does not require us to say that prayer, but instead we can say a prayer in our own words, admitting guilt and asking for God's mercy and forgiveness and resolve to sin no more and even stay away from persons, places or things that lead us to sin. A priest once said our sins are already forgiven when we come to confession; that confession is simply a Celebration of that forgiveness, if we have already repented. I believe that now deceased priest was right. SIMPLY REPENT AND RESOLVE TO SIN NO MORE! STAY AWAY FROM WHAT INVITES YOU TO SIN, IF YOU CAN!

Jesus forgave Mary Magdalene with the message that her sins were forgiven; go in peace and "sin no more".

24
Indifference

When deciding which course we take in life, we cannot "sit on the fence". We must make a decision. Which side are we on. To be indifferent means that we do not care which side we are on...that it makes no difference. However, if we are not on God's side of the fence and simply "straddle" it, we are indifferent. Indifference leads to a sin of omission—not doing what we are obligated to do. Regarding our behavior concerning God, if we are not with Him, we are against Him. There is no middle ground where we can avoid taking a stand. If we stand with God, we will find Happiness, for that is the true path for everyone with the gift of faith in God.

We should also pray that others without the gift of faith from the Holy Spirit will receive that gift and evangelize with the teachings found in the Bible and religious writings.

25
Please People or God?

Our local pastor, in a sermon not long ago, said that we should not worry about pleasing people, but try to please God. He was so right! But, God does not want us to worry about pleasing Him, but to trust Him and Love Him. We exemplify this by avoiding sin and pursuing virtue. Then, we are on our way to Heaven in this lifetime and the next. We cannot please people all the time, but we can please God by simply loving and trusting Him.

26
God is Love; Can We be Love?

St. John in his first letter in the Bible says "God is Love". God loves us. He shares Himself with us, which is His Love.

If we follow His example and become "love" ourselves, we can share ourselves—our love—with others.

By sharing this love we are not searching for love from others—only giving love. We never have to search for love from God. Unlike human love sometimes, God's love is always there for us.

27
Music: Old Songs and It's Value to People

Old songs bring back memories, sometimes, of the past. They are familiar to us unlike new songs which brings back little, if anything, in memory. The mind likes familiarity. It tends to stir up old emotions, frequently good ones, from the days gone by.

Some persons have said that old songs can be helpful to dementia patients in that it sets them back into the time before the dementia set in. In my opinion, that makes sense. What they are familiar with tends to make their uncomfortable emotions ease up because they like familiarity and actually have trouble dealing with change more than the average person does.

In conclusion, if all persons, not only those with dementia, listen to old familiar songs, they can be given a certain euphoria if the music arouses good emotions, which it can. It can bring them back emotionally to a mood that can even improve spiritual wellbeing—Happiness!

28
Invitations Rather Than Scares

I believe in inviting people to God for Happiness rather than scaring them with the punishment of Hell. Believe and trust in God because God is Love. The reward is a relationship with God, culminating in a place called Heaven after experiencing Happiness in this lifetime. Heaven is Happiness perfected—no downside!

29
Love and Helping Others

If we love people, we should try to ascertain what their needs are to help them. That can be very difficult if people do not want our help. Then, we can still pray for them. By helping or praying for others we can receive the Joy of doing something good.

30
Courage to Do Good Deeds

Sometimes we are faced with a seeming dilemma. We want to do a good deed, but are afraid of the repercussions it might cause. There is an inherent risk in doing some good deeds. Will it backfire in our face with unintended results?

However, if we believe that God values our deeds to be attempted, we can move forward with them knowing that God is with us and will reward us. Fear, though sometimes warning us of danger, is not the best motivator. Love based on Truth is the best motivator.

31
Does God Need to Earn Our Trust?

No. God does not need to earn our trust. He requests it and we are commanded to love Him. However, if anyone should doubt that, look to Christ's crucifixion with all the suffering and death that went along with it. What more could God have done than to send HIs Son to suffer and die for us? If that doesn't earn our trust, then what does? God has completely and definitely earned our trust, though He did not have to.

32
Celebrating Life

My wife used to say to me when I had some beers: "what are you celebrating?" My answer comes to me now with no guilt: "I am celebrating life." Everyday we can celebrate life itself, even if there is nothing tangible to celebrate. We can simply celebrate our prosperity, not just materially, but perhaps emotionally and spiritually. (This is in no way to promote beer drinking, but to celebrate Happiness in our own way as often as we see fit.

33
Fear and Hatred

There are times when unfounded fear can lead to hatred. People can be so afraid of something or someone that they turn to hate and try to destroy that fear by damaging or destroying what they conceive as the source of that fear

ONLY LOVE CAN DESTROY FEAR if we do not want to destroy people as the source of that fear. And we should never, ever want to destroy people or even take away their freedom, if we can use diplomacy which can lead to Love. This applies to both personal and international relations. If we think positive, we can move forward and be motivated by LOVE instead of fear.

(Of course, self-defense and national defense are OK and even necessary at times when attacked by others.)

34
Is Fun OK?

Some people believe that we were not put on this earth to have fun. Fun to them is a not acceptable. All that matters to those people is work, possibly even with no significant result of that work. To me, that is carrying the idea of the "work ethic" too far. They are cheating themselves out of enjoyment, particularly enjoyment of others. Fun can be a positive result of sharing our experiences and thoughts with others. It can be good!

Fun is related to Joy. When we do something to bring Joy to others, it can bring Joy to ourselves. Thus, Joy could be the result of fun with others or the cause of it. This Joy brings us Happiness and it can be based on fun. That leads us to GOD Who is Happiness.

35
God Loves Us

Sometimes, when I want to write, I can't think of anything to write except: "God loves me." When we are not sure what to do, we should remember that God loves us. God loves us not necessarily because we deserve it, but because, despite all our faults, it is in the nature of God, Who is actually Supernatural, to love us.

As the Apostle John said: "God is Love." To identify with Love is to identify with God. Who would not want Love? Who would not want God?

A song said: "Love is the answer." Therefore, God is the answer. And from Love comes Happiness because it comes from God. If we ask God to help us find our way, He will do so.

36
Can We Experience Happiness without Paying for it Later?

Does Happiness come with a price; that we will pay for it later? As we say about the weather: it's nice now, but wait until the "other shoe drops". Why do we sometimes have trouble accepting Happiness without believing that we will pay for it later?

I believe the answer is based on fear: the fear that good times cannot last. However, some good times can be considered Happiness, which is a gift from God. He does not want us to suffer later for it, as if we do not deserve it. If we do not deserve it, why would God give it to us? There is no downside to God and no downside to deserved Happiness. Do not assume it will end, but have Faith in God that it will continue.

37
God is There to Help Us?

Sometimes, I wish I had all the answers to every question on my mind, but I don't. However, there Is someone who does have all the answers...GOD! He has the answers to our questions and our prayers. We should PATIENTLY OPEN OUR HEARTS AND MINDS TO HIM to receive our answers.

If we trust in God, we will never go astray. We lose our way only when we fail to trust in Him. Jesus is the Way, the Truth and the Life!

38
Should We Ever Hate Ourselves for Sinning?

The second great commandment Jesus gave us is: Love our neighbor as OURSELVES. We should always love ourselves. This love is necessary for repentance when we sin. We are commanded to love ourselves, despite our sins.

39
Is Morality Absolute or Relative?

I do not believe that morality is unimportant, but I do believe it is more relative than absolute. There are degrees of morality: some really evil offenses and some not so serious. Also, there is a gray area where good meets not so good.

Still, evil does exist as well as virtue. Morality is necessary and we should, of course, avoid evil and pursue virtue.

40
Can God be Offended?

God can be offended by us. He is not simply energy, but a being who diffuses energy throughout the universe. This energy is Love. That is what is meant by God is Love.

"Beloved, let us love one another because God is Love. Everyone who loves is begotten by God and knows God. Whoever is without love does not know God, for God is Love." (1 John 7-8)

Also, we were made in God's image and likeness (Genesis). Therefore, just as we can be offended so can God be offended, like a trusted friend, who, I believe, is God.

But, God does not reject us when we sin like we sometimes do. He offers us forgiveness if we repent.

God's Love is Unconditional, unlike human love, which is often conditional.

God always loves us and offers us Happiness no matter what we do.

41
How Can We be Our Own Best Friend?

We can be our own best friend by letting God be our best friend. If God lives in us, if we let Him in, He is our best friend and we can be One with Him, but not being Him. This results in us being our own best friend. We then gain self-assurance and confidence that the decisions we make are sound, because they are founded on God, our best friend.

42
Is it OK to have a Need for Love?

Some contemporary philosophies propose that people should not have a need for love, because if we are totally "free", we will have no such needs. To me such a philosophy denies reality. In my opinion, it is a need of the "soul".

Much of this need for love can be satisfied with our love relationship with God. But, we are by nature social beings and have an inherent need for love from other humans. This is normal and should not be denied as a need. In short, we should not feel "weak" if we have a need for this love from others. However, we should also remember that giving love can also be considered a need. Giving Love can bring Us Joy which leads to Happiness. Giving love, if complimented by the bonus of receiving love results in Ultimate Happiness in this lifetime and the next. And, it all comes from giving and receiving love to and from others and/or God—the Source of All Love! God is Happiness!

43
Prayer: Politics and Government

Every day every American should pray for wisdom and understanding for our President, Vice President their Administration, our Legislators and Judges. Their success is our success. We should pray, specifically for unifying and healing this nation through the actions of all three branches of our government, both nationally and more locally (at all levels of Government). We should pray that we can reach "compromise" again rather than settle for "polarization". Hopefully, this polarization can be overcome based on the TRUTH, which comes from God. It is difficult to have true compromise if each side refuses to "listen" to each other.

Finally, we can reach compromise if each side remembers the two great commandments of Jesus Christ: Love God with all your heart, soul, mind and strength, and love you neighbor as yourself. Then, maybe, if either side does not look at the other side as the enemy, perhaps we can open our hearts and realize we are all Americans in this together. In that lies the hope for peace and unity in our great nation. God Bless the United States of America!

44
Are Humility and Self Love Related

Yes. Humility is simply being honest with ourselves about who we are. If we conclude after self-examination that we are worthy of much self-love, then we should have it. We can be who we really want to be or all that we can be, by being humble and loving ourselves.

45
Prayer and Conscience

Prayer is simply talking to God. If that prayer is Him talking to us, and it is guiding us according to sound principles, it is then a well-formed conscience. These principles could be The Ten Commandments. If our conscience is well founded, we should obey it, lest we sin. God talks to us for our benefit. He wants to steer us towards lasting Happiness.

46
Pleasing and Trusting God

It seems that God is all I need in my life. God does not speak in harsh words, but in soft loving words. If we trust God, we will please Him. Our money says: "In God we trust". I say: "In God I trust". Of course, I still do depend on family and friends for support and hope that I can continue to depend on them.

However, it has been said: "Do not put all your eggs in one basket". I say if that basket is God's basket, it is prudent to do so. People can be fickle, but God never is and can always be trusted. God is Happiness!

47
The Search for the Truth: Listening and Compromise

When we think we know it all and won't even listen to ideas or beliefs contrary to ours, we are in danger of ending our search for the Truth. This is not to say that we cannot be firm in our basic beliefs, but that we should listen to others with whom we appear to disagree. The Desiderata poem states: "Listen to others, even the dull and the ignorant. They too have their story". We do not have to agree with everything that others say, but if we listen we might find "common ground" which can lead to compromise. In a democracy such as ours it is important to reach compromise so that we can move forward as a society.

48
Jesus Before Pontius Pilate

Jesus answered Pontius Pilate with the following response from Scripture when asked about what He had done wrong when the Jewish Chief Priests had handed Him over to Pilate:

"I came into this world to testify to the Truth. Everyone who belongs to the Truth listens to my voice". Pilate said to Him: ""What is truth?" (John 18: 37,38.)

Jesus did not reply to Pilate's question about the truth and He was crucified . However, the Truth Jesus was referring to comes to us today through the Holy Spirit who is an advocate of Jesus and He can help us advocate for Jesus Christ today. If we do so, we will certainly be welcomed into Heaven when we meet Jesus right after we die. He will say: "Come, o good and faithful servant to share in the feast of my Father's table" in Heaven! However, each of us must find our own path to Heaven. There is no "one size fits all".

49
JESUS: I AM THE WAY, THE TRUTH AND THE LIFE!

Sometimes, I wish I had all the answers to every question, but I don't. But somebody does have the answers to our questions and prayers: GOD. We should open our hearts and minds to Him to receive answers. If we trust God we will never go astray. We lose our way when we fail to trust in Him. JESUS IS THE WAY, THE TRUTH AND THE LIFE! Jesus said no one goes to the Father, except through me. Therefore, accept Jesus Christ and we will be alright.

50
Loving and Accepting Jesus

If we accept Jesus and trust Him, He will be within us and we are assured Heaven if He knows us when we meet Him after our earthily lives end. He will know us by our deeds. Did we practice the Corporal Works of

Mercy? (helping with the physical needs of others) Did we do it for the "least of His brethren" and thus, do it for Him?

Jesus never rejects us. We must accept and follow Him to receive our Heavenly reward which can start right here in this lifetime. God is Happiness!

51
How is God within Us?

How is God "within us" as told by Scripture? Jesus said: "the Kingdom of God is within us." God is "within us" most notably from Scripture, but also by praying: giving and receiving messages to and from God if we are open to Him.

Also. Jesus can come to us and be within us when we receive Holy Communion. Then, His Spirit can reside in us. Also, I believe that Jesus can be within us at any time, if we open up and let Him in.

Thus, God can be within us in two ways: Word and Spirit. Both are important and can bring us to Heaven in this lifetime and the next.

52
If God Resides in Us, Does that Make us God?

NO! Let me use this example: if we have a guest into our house, we are sharing our house with them. However, that guest does not become our house or us. Like the guest, when God resides in us, we do not become God. Our bodies are "Temples of the Holy Spirit" where God resides, but the distinction between God and us is always there. We NEVER become God.

In marriage, it has been said that "the two shall become one". However, both partners are distinct from each other. Both maintain their separate identities. So it is with God. Becoming one with each other, but still separate persons. I have no better way to explain it, so I do believe that we are always separate persons.

53
Are Humility and Self Love Mutually Exclusive?

No. As I said in article 44, much less than being mutually exclusive, they are actually related. With humility we can actually love ourselves more because we are free of the false images we may have of ourself. From honesty about ourselves, we can love who we really are. That comes from humility. From humility comes Love of God, Neighbor and OURSELVES.

54
What Defines Our Relationships with Others?

What defines our relationship with others is NOT the problems between us, but solutions to those problems (or attempts at solutions) resulting many times to more togetherness or closeness.

When I think back on my life with my wife of 34 years of marriage, what comes to mind more and more is how trust and love developed right up till the day she died. This was despite all the obstacles we faced on our journey. By overcoming obstacles, we can increase our trust and love with others. OVERCOMING our obstacles with God can also have this result. OVERCOMING obstacles in our relationships define those relationships rather than the obstacles we encounter.

55
Love and Forgiveness

As explained in article 8, Love and Forgiveness go hand in hand. There cannot be one without the other. They are dependent on each other. We are all sinners, so the need for forgiveness always arises and it must be facilitated by love. Love conquers all!

56 Happiness: Divine Providence

We should never believe that we are totally responsible for our Happiness as if God played no part in it. We can earn money, but money alone does not bring happiness. It only provides that our physical needs are met. Our Emotional and Spiritual needs come from God and others. These needs can by met by loving God, Others and Ourselves.

Divine Providence is based on the "hand of cards" we have been dealt by God. If we use that "hand" wisely, we can find Happiness in this lifetime and the next. But, we must remember that God is the source of our Happiness. God is Happiness!

57
Using People

In my opinion, it is immoral to use someone and then simply discard that person if we have no further use for them. I must qualify that statement—all people use people in some fashion. Employers use people for their abilities and talents to perform for them. This, of course, is not necessarily immoral. What is immoral is to use them without regard for their needs. If an employer treats an employee fairly and cares reasonably for the employee's needs, the usage is OK. However, if an employer discerns that an employee is a detrimental to the business, then it is, of course, OK to "let the employee go", provided that it is a sound business decision and the employee is treated fairly in the dismissal, including, if possible, the welfare of the employee who was "fired". Then, there is nothing immoral about that decision.

In interpersonal relationships, we should not use someone to acquire things or even satisfy our emotional needs without considering their needs. To withdraw our love without careful consideration of another's needs can be immoral. We should not burn bridges, if possible, but should do so when both sides no longer want the relationship.

58
Integrity

Integrity is defined as honesty. I want to consider honesty in business owners' decisions. In particular what comes to mind is paying "just taxes", such as income taxes for small businesses and, possibly, even sales taxes.

It is, I believe, common for small business owners to request and receive payment in "cash" to avoid paying taxes to the government. Since that income cannot be traced, such businesses do that without fear of being caught by the government.

Consider what Jesus said about paying taxes when asked by early Jewish leaders to trap Him: "Pay unto Cesar what is Cesar's and pay unto God what is God's." So, pay "just taxes".

In conclusion, if our interest on our federal deficit exceeds our GNP, I think we face a financial problem for our nation. Everyone should pay "just" taxes to pay for necessary government spending, which can increase the federal deficit. Also, we must consider state and local government spending, which should be covered by taxation.

On the other hand, what I believe is far worse, possibly, is loopholes in our tax code for large corporations to avoid their share of taxes. Also, loopholes for wealthy persons to avoid taxes is an immoral loophole. I believe in a fair "graduated" income tax that require wealthy persons and large for-profit organizations to pay a bigger percentage of their income in taxes because they are able to do so, and, in my opinion even obligated to do so. Let's fix the tax code to make it morally just, if it is not just.

In conclusion, this nation was built on "integrity". Let's keep it that way! Integrity is an important pillar of our society. We are on sound footing and can have a sound relationship with God, if we do so. God is Happiness!

59
Consequences of Our Actions

Sometimes, some of us do things that seem justified, but we do not really consider the consequences of our actions. Considering the consequences of our actions requires wisdom. Wisdom helps us make sound decisions and it comes from God. Wisdom can bring us Happiness. God is Happiness!

60
Do We Take God for Granted?

Sometimes I think we take God for granted. That is not the same as "trusting" God. When we take God for granted we express no humility or gratitude to Him for what he has already done for us. But if we trust God, that means that we admit our weaknesses, but trust that He will help us despite those weaknesses. DO NOT TAKE GOD FOR GRANTED! TRUST HIM! DOING SO GIVES US HOPE FOR HAPPINESS!

61
God's Plan for Us

God has a plan for us, though in our darker moments we may not realize it. God will never abandon us and we should never abandon Him.

The Desiderata poem reads: "The universe is unfolding as it should." It does so because God created the universe and has the plan for its unfolding. My Mom used to say: "God has a plan". Many years later I agree. If we trust in Him, our plan will be His plan, and all will work out to our advantage.

62
Making Excuses for Sinning

At times, after committing a sin, we try to make excuses to justify what we have done, instead of apologizing to the one against whom we committed the sin, if possible, and to God and asking for His forgiveness. Admitting guilt rather than simply making excuses is the only prudent road to forgiveness and reconciliation with others and with God. From reconciliation comes opportunity for Happiness, for God is Happiness!

63
What is Accomplishment?

Too often, I think we consider accomplishment as the visible product of what we have worked for. What comes to mind for me, is the finished product of my work on this book I am writing,

However, there are many other forms of accomplishment. Consider conversing with others even in phone or text messages. Consider prayer—talking to God. These certainly should be considered accomplishment.

Exercise can be considered accomplishment, either in the form of a shoveled driveway after shoveling snow, or simply walking or working out on a treadmill or other exercise equipment

All types of work can be considered accomplishments as well as some leisure activities, such as fishing, even if no fish are caught.

Contemplation or meditation can be considered accomplishment. It is not being idle when we perform those mental activities, though we may think it is at times.

Thus, accomplishment can come in many forms and lead to satisfaction in life and Happiness. The motivation to do those things comes from God, from Whom all good things come. God is Happiness!

64
Trust and Jesus

Jesus said : "No greater love is there than for one to lay down one's life for His friends." The dictionary defines trust as: "confident reliance on the integrity, honesty or justice of another's faith". Trust can be taking a "leap of faith for someone".

It has been said : "love makes the world go round". However, trust also "makes the world go round". Without trust our social and economic system would collapse. Imagine not trusting in business relationships, the stocks market (for honesty) and international relations, which is a difficult arena for trust but still important among allies.

Finally, I believe trust in God is the most important type of trust and the foundation of all trust, Jesus laid down Him life for us. He deserves our trust, and actually wants us as a trusted friend.

65
God the Father

Contemporary religions, both denominational and non-denomination, certainly do give a lot of attention to Jesus. But, we should also give utmost attention to Jesus's Father. Jesus gave us the Lord's Prayer or the "Our Father". Jesus told us to pray directly to the Father in that prayer. It was HIs Father's will to which He willingly succumbed to death on the cross: Jesus said: "thy will, not mine be done" in the Garden the night before His death.

The Our Father says "give us this day our daily bread and forgive us our trespasses". Thus, we should ask the Father, not just Jesus, for our needs including our need for forgiveness. In my opinion, the Father is Jesus's boss. Jesus said the Father is greater than the Son. However, He also said, no one goes to the Father except though the Son. I interpret this to mean Jesus is the "gatekeeper", who approves or denies us the passage into His Father's Heavenly Kingdom after we die.

66
Can We Become Saints?

It is my belief that some of us become Saints in this lifetime without even knowing it or other people knowing it. They may seem very simple persons, who may not have many, if any, "notable" achievements. They probably do not suffer martyrdom like some apostles probably did. But, God knows they are saints and His Son, Jesus, knows it too. So, Jesus invites them into the many mansions of His Father's house after these Saints die on earth. Thus, they receive the Happiness they deserve. We too can become Saints if we follow Jesus closely by avoiding sin and pursuing virtue. Then, Jesus will invite us to the Heavenly Kingdom.

67
Anger and Humility

Anger, usually, if not always, comes from feeling that we have been hurt by someway and so we seek revenge or punishment against them. But, anger, which Jesus warned against, comes from pride. Some persons who make us angry may even be trying to help us. Have the humility to listen, instead of becoming angry. With humility, we may not be so judgmental, which Jesus also warned against. Regarding anger, Jesus said that he who is even angry will be liable to judgment, I think, from God. Finally, anger can lead to damaging actions—a terrible outcome! We must have the humility to listen and "cool off" when beginning to feel anger, so we do what we really want to do.

All of this is not to say that we cannot defend ourselves if attacked blatantly and unjustly by others.

68
Is It Judgmental to Criticize Other Person's Actions?

No. It is not judgmental to criticize others actions. For example, they may embellish or "fudge" the truth. Do not judge them, but only their actions if we think criticizing such behavior will help them. Thus, constructive criticism is good. From such criticism can come positive discussion on ways for them to improve.

In conclusion, Jesus said: "woe to you that judge, lest you be judged." So, judge or criticize another's actions, but not the person, if that is possible. Being non-judgmental towards others will lead both you and them closer to God, from Whom all Virtue comes.

69
Jesus: Are We Just LUKEWARM for Him?

Jesus said: "I would rather you be hot or cold. If you are lukewarm, I would like to vomit you right out of my mouth". This is a strong statement asking for enthusiasm and excitement when talking about Jesus or doing things in His name.

I am, by nature, an excitable person. Some persons may view that as a weakness, but I believe it depends what I am excited about. After starting to write my books, I felt excitement when discussing matters concerning Jesus Christ and the Truth He offered. I certainly do not want Him to vomit me right out of His mouth for being a lukewarm follower of His. I also do not want anyone to be lukewarm for Jesus for that reason. BE HOT FOR JESUS! DO NOT BE JUST LUKEWARM. Try to find some way to express your beliefs in Him to further His cause with enthusiasm. Doing so may bring you Joy and, ultimately, Happiness! God is Happiness!

70
Who was Jesus?

It is my belief that Jesus was so humble that He did not claim to be equal to God. However, His presence is everywhere with all the Christian Churches. Christian Churches have attempted to define His Divinity with the Concept of the Blessed Trinity. It states that there are three persons in one God. I believe whether these three person are equal persons is up for debate. Anyway, the Trinity is still a mystery.

What is important to me is that Jesus is the Son of God, both Divine and Human. I believe that His performing of miracles: healing of the sick, multiplying the loaves and fishes, changing water into wine and much more, probably some of which is not even recorded in Scripture, point to His importance to mankind. Ultimately, his passion and death on the cross with the resulting Resurrection prove His love for mankind. Then, the Holy Spirit which He sent to His apostles on Pentecost started the spreading of the word about Him and the beginning of Christianity. It is my belief that He has done more for mankind than any other single person. He has made it possible to obtain true lasting Happiness!

71
Spiritual Love

In my first romantic, but celibate, relationship with a woman in college, I said to her that I had a Spiritual Love for her. She dismissed it with: Oh, ya. Perhaps, she wanted a more physically intimate relationship than I was ready for.

Nevertheless, I believe Spiritual Love does exist. With Spiritual Love we are Soulmates for each other and go beyond physical intimacy and even emotional bonding. It can include praying for the other. As Soulmates, we are bound together for eternity, though not married in Heaven where Jesus said there are no marriages.

I am waiting to join my Soulmate, who is my wife of 34 years, passing away and entering the Kingdom of Heaven a few years ago. Contemplating that reunion with her brings Hope, Peace, and Happiness to me.

72
Non-Christian Religions

I have said in my earlier book "God is Love" that if we reject Jesus, we bar ourselves from Heaven; to keep the door open to Heaven, keep the door open to Jesus.

I have also said in my book "Thoughts and Writings" that as long as religions and philosophies stress the importance of love, we can work together for peace and love among all peoples.

The issue is: Do non-Christians reject Jesus or simply deny that He was Divine, but perhaps a prophet or only a philosopher? Or, perhaps, they are not familiar with Jesus at all.

In my opinion, such persons are not barred from Heaven. However, it may be a different sort of Heaven that they enter after living a good life. However, if someone knows Jesus and rejects Him permanently, I do believe that he/she is barred from Heaven.

I believe the soul is eternal, at least for those who believe in some Superior being. Regarding agnostics and atheists, it is not for us to judge. Only God know if those souls should continue to live on in some sort of Heaven after they die. It is my prayer that all persons turn to a belief in God before they die. God is Happiness!

73
Resurrection of the Dead: Heaven and Hell

Until the time of Christ, the idea of everlasting life was not clear. Jesus offered everlasting life—something new—I believe. However, many Jews probably did believe in the Resurrection of the Dead, unlike the Sadducees who denied it.

With the Resurrection of Jesus Christ, the Resurrection of the Dead took on new meaning because Jesus showed that the Resurrection was possible. Thus, His promise of everlasting life was proven. Jesus was given the keys to Death and Hell, and I believe the keys to Heaven and is still today the "gatekeeper" who judges us after we die to decide if we can enter Heaven.

Hell is simply the grave to me —the "netherworld" or the underground where our bodies or ashes are buried after we die. The " fires of Hell" was a garbage dump outside Jerusalem at the time of Christ where criminals or just dead bodies were thrown, I believe. (Mt 5:29; 10:28; 18:8f; Mk 9:44ff) It was known as Gehenna and was considered "Hell" at that time.

There are no "fires of Hell" today. The only way we could enter the netherworld or Hell is if we do NOT choose everlasting life through belief in Jesus. Then, it could be that we lie there in the casket until Christ comes to raise the dead at the final Resurrection of the Dead. If we believe in Jesus Christ's promise of everlasting life, we enter Heaven immediately after the soul leaves the body after death, if Jesus admits us. The soul has no reason for going to the grave in the cemetery if it believed in Jesus and is admitted to Heaven by Him. If so, then, no one is in the casket, for the soul is in Heaven.

74
Count Our Blessings

When things seem to be going bad for us, we should pause and consider what is going right for us. We should count our blessings.

My Dad used to tell me to look at the positive rather than the negative. I will never forget his advice on that matter. It has helped me thwart worry and fear so much.

75
Good Times: Trust in God

I have said in my book: " God is Love" that we should have faith in God that, if we are in "good times" that this will continue rather than being fearful that it will end. Good times do not come with the price that we will pay for it later. All goodness comes from God. Trust that He will bring us Happiness!

76
God Answers Our Prayers

A while ago, I prayed to God to reconnect with an old girlfriend from the early adult years. I now am realizing that God's answer to that prayer is that it is probably more trouble than it is worth, so the prayer was, I believe, answered with a NO. Even "no" is an answer, though most people probably do not consider that to be true.

God knows what we need. If we accept what He gives us rather than complaining to Him, we will be much happier. GOD GIVES US WHAT WE NEED, BUT NOT NECESSARILY WHAT WE DESIRE. Desires can be off God's path for us and lead us into much unhappiness.

If God answers our prayers with a Yes that means that answer will keep us on God's path or plan for us. At times, it can even bring us back to God's path if we have strayed away from it.

At times, we do not know if our desires are also needs. We will know the answer to that question by the way God answers our prayer—either a YES or NO. God gives us what we NEED, not just to physically survive, but to be Happy. GOD IS HAPPINESS!

77
What is Laziness?

I have said that accomplishment can be many things, even leisure activities such as fishing. Laziness, to me is turning away from virtuous acts which we recognize, but avoid, not because we are fatigued, but because we want to have fun. To me accomplishment from fun is less important than accomplishment from truly virtuous acts.

We should always do our best to accomplish virtuous acts. Fun has as time and place. To quote the Bible: "There is a time for everything under the sun". So there is a time for fun, but if we see a need for real virtue, we should not be "lazy", but attempt the more important virtuous act instead of fun. Let God guide us to Joy from good deeds leading to Happiness, rather than temporary fun.

78
Karma: What Goes Around Comes Around

The statement above describes what Karma means to me. What we do comes back to us either in reward or suffering (possibly mental or emotional). Good deeds bring rewards; evil deeds bring some type of suffering. Such outcomes cannot be avoided.

If we suffer in some other way for doing evil, what is important to remember is that God does not desert us after we do so. He offers an "olive branch" of peace to reconcile with Him. After reconciliation, there can be only peace and, I believe, Happiness, for God is Happiness!

79
Humility, Admitting When We Are Wrong

If a person is so proud that he/she cannot admit wrongdoing, he/she lacks humility and damage their relationship with others and God. It shows false pride.

Also, if someone does not have an answer to some question from another, they should admit that instead of offering an answer that is not well founded, just to appear "smart". I think I have been guilty of that at times and must resolve never to do it again. It takes humility to say to a person asking a question: "I do not know". After doing so, we can turn to God to find an answer through prayer and/or research. Prayer is based on humility and can bring us Happiness.

80
Jesus: His Ascension into Heaven and His Second Coming

Jesus said before He ascended into Heaven in front of His Apostles: I will be with you until the end of time......you will see the Son of Man coming down from the sky just as you saw Him leaving. This points to Christ's second coming.

It could be He has already come to some of us in various ways. I heard a story about a hitchhiker who got in the back seat of a car and asked if the driver knew about the "second coming of Christ". Then, when the driver turned to view the passenger hitchhiker, he had disappeared. I do not know if the story was true or not.

However, I had a similar experience many years ago, but with a "helper" who flagged down a car for me, for I was out in a field after falling asleep and running off the road and unable to start my car. I did not know what to do when a person walking along the side of the highway smiled at me, so I walked up to Him and explained my situation. Then He flagged down a car for me and instantly DISAPPEARED. When I got into the car, which he had flagged down, I looked back and he was there again, smiling at me. Was that JESUS I do not know, but I believe it was at least an ANGEL. Whatever or Whoever you were, I do not believe I really thanked YOU until now.

THANK YOU!

81
Health of the Soul

Health of the Body and Mind is what is often considered Health. However, Health of the Soul is important too. It comes from efforts to gain wisdom on a virtuous road of Love of God, neighbor and ourselves. It could be that health of the soul, promoted by prayer, could do more to bring us Happiness than exercise and healthy food. Health of the soul is nourished by meditation on religious topics and a sense of peace that can come from that contemplation.

Finally, a sense of Humor is necessary for Health of the Soul. If we are so serious much of the time, it could be that we have lost or never had a sense of Humor to put our lives into proper priorities. Thus, we do not "sweat the small stuff" with this perspective. Then we can laugh at "small potatoes" of problems. Remember to laugh if you want to be happy.

82
Order: The First Law of the Universe?

While working with a counselor on the VISTA program (Volunteers in Service to America) helping to counsel inmates on job seeking upon release from a minimum security prison, the counselor I was assisting said to me : "Order is the First Law of the Universe". I was not sure of the truth of that statement back then, but now realize it is true. The "Universe is unfolding as it should", as explained in the Desiderata poem. It is unfolding as it should because God is unfolding it.

While working at Post Offices for 22 years, I learned that there is a place for all the mail pieces. Thus, there had to be order for the mail to be sorted properly for delivery. Those years of work have taught me the value of "Order". Keeping that order in our relationship to God is important. Structured religious beliefs and prayers are certainly important in our relationship with God. However, we may explore other ways of worshipping God and can, sometimes, find new ways leading to a new order of relating to God. However, without some order it is difficult to relate to God, even on a personal level. The "old ways" may be boring at times, but sometimes the old ways can be trusted and true. We must all find our "true" way to Heaven and the Happiness it brings us.

83
Regrets: Do They Have Value?

Although, I have said in "Thoughts and Writings" that we should not "stew over the past", I believe that regrets about the past can bring us wisdom. If we have reason to regret something we did in the past, we can learn from that experience to promise that we will never do it again. Then, we get back on the road to virtue which leads us to Heaven wherein Happiness lies, beginning in this current lifetime.

84
Humility: Self Love and Loving Others

I have said in "Thoughts and Writings" that the more we love ourselves, the more we are required to love others: love "others" as "ourselves". Humility is the virtue from which we can learn to know ourselves honestly. When we practice this virtue, we can love ourselves more based on that knowledge. Humility is not self-hatred, but can bring increased self-love and loving others. Also, through humility, we can love God more and attain Happiness based on that love and love of others.

85
God is Love: Regrets and Forgiveness

I have regrets concerning my life, and complain about others at times, but I certainly do forgive everyone who has offended me. So my complaints are just "venting" with no malice intended against the other who has offended me in some way. It is my prayer that I leave this world in the good graces of God and everyone.

86
Fear of the Lord: A Gift of the Holy Spirit

This gift of the Holy Spirit has puzzled me. I view God as a trusted friend. Why should I fear Him? I believe that this "fear" from this "gift" was mentioned in the Old Testament, when the early Hebrews thought of God as a punishing God. That was the theme at that time. It was meant to increase faith in God. Since Jesus Christ, however, the New Testament views God as more loving and forgiving.

Today, my belief is that God is even more benevolent yet. I view "fear of the Lord" as fearing to offend Him not because He will punish us, but we will punish ourselves if we offend God. We threaten our own fate by turning away from God. Also, I do not want to offend God because it could cause Him pain or discomfort. I do not know, but certainly want to avoid that if it does exist.

Finally, it is not that God has changed through the ages, but that our "view" of God has changed. I think we are closer to seeing the "real God" today than we were in the days of the Old Testament. Progress has been made and it can bring us more Happiness than ever before. God is Happiness.

87
My Testimony and Religion

I believe that I am a freelance writer for God and Mankind. I do not consider myself a spokesman for any Church, Christian or Non-Christian. I do believe in Salvation through Jesus Christ, so I am a Christian. Also, I was raised a Catholic and still consider myself a Catholic, so I am naturally biased towards that religion. However, as I have said in "Thoughts and Writings", I believe that all religions that stress Love and Peace have value. My desire is to proclaim God's "contemporary" word to mankind, though I do not claim my words to be the "word of God", Who brings me great Joy and Happiness in my writings and books. It is my desire that my books do that for others, also.

88
Respect

I have said in "Thoughts and Writings" and "God is Love" that all persons deserve love and respect. With regard to respect, all persons deserve respect as in "respect for Life".

However, there is another type of respect that is earned based on some achievement a person has made to earn respect from others. That "respect" is fine, but the danger is that such respect will lead to excessive pride and even "snobbishness. We must maintain humility, especially when honored by others for our achievements. From humility comes Happiness in a sound relationship with God and Others.

89
God: Love and Suffering

"God is Love". God does not want anyone to suffer. He does not enjoy watching suffering. Not only does God not enjoy watching suffering, He is moved to compassion by it, not indifferent to it, as some persons believe because He allows it. Jesus had enough compassion to heal the sick, feed the hunger and even raise the dead. More recently, God had compassion on those living in the age of Covid19. I believe He inspired medical researchers to invent the Covid19 vaccine which has been successful in slowing the infection. From that vaccine we can return to some sense of "normalcy in our lives.

God cares. God is Happiness.

90
Why Did Christ Die on the Cross?

A Christian belief is that Jesus Christ died as atonement to God, His Father, for the sins of mankind. I find that belief difficult for me to believe. Sacrifice to God dates back to the Old Testament when animals were killed and presented to God as appeasement or offerings in order to be forgiven of sins or reconciled to God. It was meant to show, according to Hebrews or Jews as they are now called, the love they had for God.

My view of God is that He no longer wants or is pleased with such offerings. Thus, re-sacrificing Jesus every time the Catholic Church offered the "Holy Sacrifice of the Mass" makes no sense to me. I do not claim to know if that belief still is prominent in the Catholic Church, but I cannot support it. St. Paul said Jesus died "once " and no more.

It is my opinion that Jesus lived and died for us to show us true humility. He said: "No greater love is there than one to lay down his life for his friends". He also said in the garden before he was crucified. "Father please remove this cup from me, but thy will, not mine be done." That showed great humility.

Thus, I believe that Jesus lived and died to show us a perfect model to imitate in our lives. Jesus wants us to "follow Him", but few of us need to be martyrs like some of the Saints. We can follow Jesus by defending Him and evangelizing for Him without becoming Martyrs. We should simply be Hot for Jesus and not just lukewarm. Then, we can find true Happiness for God is Happiness.

91
Penance: Interior and Exterior

Interior penance is avoiding sin and pursuing virtue with Hope for God's mercy based on our humility. Exterior penance can mean fasting, prayer and giving to others as charity; thus, giving back to God.

Both these types of penance are good and valid expressions of our desire to became better persons for God's sake. However, I do not believe that we must do penance if it means doing "favors" to God to be forgiven of sin. I do not believe that external penance is necessary if it includes doing these "favors" to God. God's love is unconditional as is His forgiveness. We do not have to appease Him with favors to be forgiven of sin. This is not to say that we cannot "want" to perform deeds and do so out of our love for Him. I am simply saying it is not necessary for forgiveness.

Also, God does not expect us to do "penance" for those sins after being forgiven. I do not believe in "indulgences" (commonly, saying certain prayers or religious reading) to lessen punishment from forgiven sins after we die. Martin Luther criticized the Catholics Church centuries ago for requiring members to "pay money" to the Church to be relieved of punishment from sins after dying. Thus, He disagreed with the Catholic Church, likely among other things, i.e., infallibility and leadership of the Pope, which led to the Reformation resulting in the Protestant Churches we have today.

It is my belief that interior penance is more important than exterior penance. However, I agree that prayer and fasting are good forms of exterior penance and can lead to Happiness in this lifetime, not just the next.

92
Happiness and Material Goods

I have said (article 35–"God is Love) that we should not assume that good times will end, Life should not be like weather. "It is nice now, but wait until the other shoe drops". We should have faith that good times will continue. I have also said: "we should not put all our eggs in one basket", except if it is in God's basket.

If we put "all our eggs" in the basket of material goods, we may be let down. Those eggs could easily rot or be stolen. The Happiness of good times can occur without much material goods, if we trust God.

The Bible says not to store up all of our treasures in material possessions which can rot or be stolen. Store up your treasures in Heaven where they cannot be taken away. Material goods are meant to serve us—not for us to serve them. Jesus said the Kingdom of Heaven is within us—therefore, not tied to any material goods. This "Kingdom within Us" can bring us Happiness in this lifetime and the next. God is Happiness.

93
Morning and Evening Prayer

Each morning, in general, I thank God for granting me another day and ask for His guidance to do His will that day just started. However, I often forget to thank God for the day just gone by. I believe it is important to thank God for the day just ending. As a child I considered that my most important time of private prayer—at my bedside praying at day's end. It was so important to me as taught by my parents. I have lost the practice of kneeling by my bed until recently, at times, though I still kept praying. Was that practice meant only for children? I do not think so. Kneeling shows humility, which can be helpful in prayer. If we forget humility, we forget God. We must remember to humbly pray if we want Happiness based on our relationships with God. God is Happiness!

94
Happiness from Within

We need to be happy alone to be truly happy in the company of others. If we place all our desires for Happiness in the hands of another person or persons, we jeopardize our freedom and happiness.

To give love to others, we must first love ourselves not the other way around. That is, we should not have all our self-love based on love for or from others. Happiness comes from giving of ourself—based on our self-love—giving love to others.

The ultimate source of all love is God. Only by loving God, Others and OURSELVES will be happy. God is Happiness because God is Love.

95
God Help Us

Once I said to a co-worker when he had a problem: "God help you". He reacted negatively that I meant only God could help Him. What I meant was not with that negative connotation, but that God is always there to help us, if we just ask Him. We do not need to begin to feel that the situation is almost hopeless to ask for God's help. God is always there to help us, not just in times of desperation.

God is Love; therefore, God is Happiness!

96
Has God Changed?

In reading the Old Testament, we find that Yahweh, the name for God at that time, was a jealous and vengeful God. Furthermore, He was a punishing God who inflicted suffering or at least allowed it as payback for disobeying Him in His many Commandments, particularly the Ten Commandments.

Later, came Jesus whose presence was foretold by the Prophet Isiah in the Old Testament.

Jesus, through His example of love by suffering and dying on the cross, gave us a new view of God—more Loving and Forgiving. Jesus condensed all the Commandments offered in the Old Testament to just two: Love God and Our Neighbor as Ourselves.

I do NOT believe that God has changed, but that our view or image of Him has changed. Jesus has simplified our approach to a positive commandment to Love. If we suffer due to sin, it is our own doing, as it was with the Hebrews in the Old Testament. However, the Apostle John wrote something "New", I believe, in HIs New Testament letter stating that God is Love: "Beloved, let us love one another because God is love. Everyone who loves is begotten by God and knows God. Whoever is without love does not know God, for GOD IS LOVE". I go further to say that GOD IS HAPPINESS!

97
My Prayer

Lord, make me an instrument of your Love, Peace and Inspiration to serve You and Others.

98
Do We Pre-Judge People?

Sometimes, I prejudged people before they even had a chance to say or do anything concerning that prejudgment. Jesus said: "Woe to you that judge lest you be judged." I believe it is wrong to prejudge people based on our prejudices. Such prejudging defeats love itself. It certainly shows no empathy. Instead of prejudging others, we should try to love them with an open mind as God loves them.

99
Is there Value in Anticipation?

Anticipating something good that we believe will happen can be a source of hope for us. Also, it can bring us patience if we trust that the good event will occur.

Anticipating our ultimate hope—Heaven, which can begin in this lifetime—can bring us happiness. God is Happiness!

100
Should We Strive for Perfection?

It has been said: "None of us are perfect". I clarify to say: "Only God is perfect". However, we should still strive for perfection, even knowing that we may never achieve it concerning perfection of our souls to become saints in this lifetime. The most important quality to perfect is Love; that is, Love of God and Our Neighbor as Ourselves. If this pursuit is based on our search for the Truth in life—Jesus Christ—we can make a difference in life. The reward for making a difference in life can be Happiness in this lifetime and the next.

God is Happiness!

101
Anger and Forgiveness

When I think of my now deceased parents and my deceased wife, it brings back memories of how good they were to me, but not only to me but to other persons they met on their journey through life. They certainly have helped me and others on our journey through life.

However, I do also remember how they hurt my feelings with what they did and said. They succumbed to anger if I unintentionally upset them in some way. I must realize now that was a "temper" issue. I have dealt with my "bad temper" towards others as well during my life. Thus, I have succumbed to anger also.

We must empathize with those who angrily have hurt us. We must try to get to know them better so that we can know what made them angry. Then, it is easier to forgive them, if we have not already done so. Nobody is perfect, including myself. Tolerance does NOT mean condoning, but simply overlooking the pain others cause to us or forgiving them.

The "Our Father" or Lord's Prayer says: "forgiven us our trespasses as WE FORGIVE THOSE WHO TRESPASS AGAINST US". I interpret "trespass" to mean "sin". If God can forgive us, we should always forgive others, for God is Love. Therefore, God is Happiness—the "Fruit" of Forgiveness!

102
God is Love: Forgiveness

The main power of God is Love. From this Love comes forgiveness. I cannot stress enough how important forgiveness is in interpersonal relationships, even to include relationships, not only in our personal lives, but in the lives of those in society to include business persons, not only in management, but those in service occupations, (hospitality and medical) and those in government, even in international relations, and volunteers in every walk of life. Forgiveness is needed to make and maintain world peace. Forgiveness manifests Love: Love of God and Others.

It is the true path for Peace on earth and Happiness based on Love of God.

103
Giving the Gift Back to God

I have said that "today" is a gift ("Thoughts and Writings"). Let me qualify to say it is a gift of Love from God. If we offer it back to Him through prayer and good works, it is still a gift, but from us to Him. We must have humility and express gratitude to Him to do so and bring us closer to Him and, therefore, receive the Happiness He offers us.

104
St. Michael the Archangel

St. Michael the Archangel is a protector from the supposed attacks and snares of the "devil". The name "Michael" means : "who is like God?" It is a question. I interpret this question to be answered with "no one is like God" completely for He is the Supreme Being. However, a depiction of the Archangel Michael is that of Him with a scale, weighing souls. I believe that to mean that if our souls are "like God" in that we Love God above all else and all others as ourselves, then we are "like God" and allowed into Heaven if approved by Jesus, the gatekeeper when we leave this earth. We should always remember to pray to St. Michael. He is the patron saint of so many different walks of life, including, I believe store owners and military personnel. He is my patron saint.

105
Why Is Trusting Others So Difficult for Us Sometimes?

To me, the main reason I have trouble trusting others is that "they have let me down" to lead me to believe that they are not trustworthy. The problem with that conclusion is that, like in the stock market, past performance is not necessarily a predictor of future performance. We must realize that, despite the past behavior of persons, we do not know their future behavior.

I believe that if we trust God, we were more likely to give others more of a chance to trust. We should not "blindly" trust others, but, I believe, at times, we should "take a leap of faith" to trust others with some risk to ourselves, especially is there is much to be gained from taking the risk if things work out right. Nobody is 100% trustworthy except God, but we should attempt to trust others as much as we can. Love, respect and trust make the world go round.

106
Does God ever Apologize to Us?

God never apologizes to us for anything, because God is perfect and never needs to apologize. However, God does understand us and wants us to know that so that we do not fear Him, for He always is on our side if we are on His side. This "understanding" is a gift from the Holy Spirit God offers us. It can bring us Happiness.

107 Prayer: Should it ever be Work?

To me, prayer is simply talking to God and listening to His answer. It does not have to be difficult or considered "work". Unlike an unpleasant job, it should be enjoyable. Also, we do not need to follow structured prayers all the time, but can speak to God in our own words.

Also, we do not need to list a litany of details when asking God for something. Jesus said God knows what we want even before we ask Him. Finally, we should not repeat the same prayers over and over again. God hears us the first time. Prayer does not have to be a chore, but instead a conversation with a trusted friend. Viewing it that way frees us up for true Happiness from God.

108
Forgiveness and Trust: Hope for Mankind

I have said that without forgiveness there is no hope for the sinner. Jesus said He came to save the world, not to condemn it. (Article 63, God is Love). Unless people turn to God for forgiveness, it is difficult for them to turn to others for forgiveness after offending them. Forgiveness offers us hope for a brighter future. It does not mean forgetting offenses to God and others. On the contrary, we should reflect on those sins to never commit them again, especially if those sins caused great damage to God and Others.

On a larger scale, mankind has waged war since the beginning of recorded history. Maybe these were not "all out" wars at times, but conflicts. Nations should try to forgive each other to move forward with peace and love. Hate and revenge too often result in war. War is based on distrust between nations. The extremes damage of war was exemplified by the atomic bombing of Hiroshima and Nagasaki which ended World War Two with Japan. I do not claim to judge the morality of those final attacks, but it clearly showed us the dangers of nuclear war.

Trust built on Love and Truth is the cement that can hold mankind together to avoid war if we possibly can. Practice diplomacy if possible. It is our hope for peace, if we can do it.

109
Are We, Today, Responsible for the Passion and Death of Christ?

NO! We were NOT living then, so how could we be responsible? The ones most responsible were the Jewish church leaders and those Jews that supported them at that time. Then, of course, Pilate washed his hands, symbolizing that it was not His sin to crucify Jesus, because some of those Jews were threatening to riot, which could cause considerable damage to the society for which Pilate was responsible as Governor. Finally, the Roman soldiers did the actually inflicting of pain and death on Jesus, but they were simply following Pilate's orders, just as soldiers follow their leaders' orders today in warfare. Some Roman soldiers went even further, however, by insulting and verbally tormenting Jesus, which was, I believe, not a necessary part of Pilate's order. But, one Roman centurion praised Jesus: "Truly this was a good man". Jesus said before He died on the cross: "Forgive them, for they know not what they do." That, I believe, was a statement meant primarily for the Roman soldiers, but it is not clear to me what He meant. Anyway, since we were not living at that time, WE ARE NOT RESPONSIBLE for the passion and death of Christ. This statement does not mean that He did not die for us, which He Did to prove His love for us and give to us a role model to follow.

110
The Freedom to Love

Once we know the truth, we are set free and can love with no prejudices. We have the words of Jesus: "Love one another as I have loved you", which He said to HIs apostles when He knew He would not be with them in physical body after ascending into Heaven.

However, He also said: "Heaven and Earth shall pass away, but my Words shall never pass away." I believe His words from the New Testament are at least 2,000 years old. Those words show no indication to me of "passing away". Also, He is within us in Spirit , if we believe in Him. He will remain with His believers forever.

Jesus is Love as God is Love. He offers Everlasting Life to those who believe in Him, which can begin as Happiness in this lifetime and the next. God is Happiness!

111
Life: Going through a Maze

A graduate school professor once said to the class: Life is like going through a "maze"—a series of paths that, if followed correctly can lead to coming out of the maze, instead of being lost in it. It is my belief that his analogy is correct. However, he did not say how we actually get ourselves out of the maze. That seems to be done trying different paths until accidentally coming out of it or trying to eliminate all paths until we find the right one.

There is someone who can lead us out of the "maze" of life—Jesus Christ! Faith and trust in Him lead to His promised everlasting life, for He is the Way, the Truth and the Life!

However, while in the "maze", we should try to eliminate the paths that lead nowhere—that lead us away from Jesus and, thus, keep us lost in the maze. If we follow Jesus, we will exit it. Then, we will find freedom through following his example of love and humility. Surrender to God and we cannot lose!

112
Does Jesus Remain in Us when We Sin?

No. Jesus leaves us when we sin, not because He wants to, but because we "kick Him out". But He does not reject us, but offers us an "olive branch" of peace and forgiveness so that we can be forgiven and reconciled to Him. If we admit our guilt and accept His forgiveness, we can gain the Happiness that He offers because He is "living in us" again.

113
What if a Companion?

I told my wife that I married her for Companionship for life. (Based on Love, of course). Thus, I married her for more than romantic love with all the "dreams" that come with romantic love. The Companionship I refer to is an act of the will, not just dreams and feelings. This "willful" love carried our relationship to the end of her earthly life: "till death do us part". Romance usually fades with time, but Love, even in Companionship, need not. It can bring true Happiness.

114
The Old Testament

The Old Testament centers on the Covenant between the Hebrews and God. Their God, or Yahweh had a Covenant with these Hebrews that they must keep to be in God's favor against their military enemies.

Yahweh promised a new land to the Chosen people if they keep the Covenant. If they should break it, as they did at times, they would suffer at the hands of their enemies who worked politically and militarily against the Hebrews who were trying to claim and maintain the "promised land". The lesson in all of this is that WE WILL SUFFER IF WE DISOBEY GOD. But, Yahweh was a jealous and punishing God in the Old Testament, unlike what followed in the New Testament with the coming of Jesus Christ.

115
The New Testament

Jesus Christ fulfilled the prophesies of the Old Testament (Isaiah) but was mostly rejected by the Jewish leads of the time (except Nicodemus and maybe others). Jesus upset the rule of the Jewish leaders very much at that time. However, His many miracles and preaching caused Him to be popular with the masses of people who witnessed Him. That upset the Jewish religious leaders even more, for they feared He could become more influential than themselves.

So, He was crucified to satisfy those Jewish leaders and their followers.

However, with the Resurrection of Jesus from the dead, we move towards the "Life" story of the New Testament. Jesus beat death, and wants us to beat death too, not that our earthly bodies won't die, but that our souls will be with Him in Heaven when our earthly bodies die. This "Heaven" can start in this lifetime with Happiness, for God is Happiness!

116
Does Jesus Ever Want Us to Hate Ourselves?

Jesus said for us to Hate our Lives: "Whoever loves his life will lose it, and whoever hates His life will save it. Does He mean that we should Hate Ourselves?

NO! Hate our Lives if our lives are miserable or even simply unpleasant, but do not hate ourselves. Jesus said Love your neighbor as YOURSELF. Therefore, He commands us to Love Ourselves.

If we stray from what God wants for us, we will suffer. Then, if we do not turn back to God, our lives will be miserable or, at least, unsatisfactory. Hate our sins, but not Ourselves to find Happiness in Life. We must always be striving to live a better life, not being simply complacent. There is always room for improvement. Hate what you do not like about your life in order to improve it to find TRUE HAPPINESS which comes from God. God is Happiness!

117
NEVER say "go to hell" to anyone!

Think about what "go to hell" literally means when you say it to someone. It means that you want someone to lose their relationship with God and suffer from that. Words matters, not just deeds, especially angry words. It is a terrible statement and requires repentance and forgiveness from God. It does not lead to Happiness and some say "go to hell" without considering how the other person interprets it. Wish Heaven, NOT Hell for everyone. In that lies Happiness.

118
Patience and Anger

I have said that patience is needed to overcome our need for immediate gratification or immediate results from our efforts. Patience is also needed to avoid violence towards another who has offended us. It is best, at times, to "bite your tongue" or "hold back your temper" if someone has hurt us in word or deeds.

Patience can modify or even eliminate ANGER if someone offends us. Then, we can stay in God's good graces and find His Happiness for us.

119
Is the Law Meant to Serve Us or for Us to Serve the Law?

Man made laws were meant to serve us by providing rules for a civil and peaceful society. We should not serve the laws, but the laws should serve us. We are a nation of people, not only a nation of laws. People make decisions including the decision to forgive offenses. Man made laws tend to be more "black and white" often not considering individual differences or circumstances.

God's Law is superior to man-made law, which finds its basic foundation in God's law. Jesus gave us His two laws of Love of God, and our Neighbor as Ourselves. Both God's laws and man-made laws are meant to create and maintain Order and Peace in our society. The Declaration of Independence was founded on God's Law to give us the opportunity and right for the "pursuit of Happiness". God is Happiness!

120
The Fruits and Gifts of the Holy Spirit

These are the Fruits of the eternal glory of the Holy Spirit: Charity, Joy, Peace, Patience, Kindness, Goodness, Generosity, Gentleness, Faithfulness, Modesty, Self-Control, and Chastity. Notice that there are twelve fruits and that they are all virtues or the result of virtues (Joy, Peace). Notice that Integrity is not included. Perhaps, this virtue is necessary to obtain the Fruits of the Holy Spirit as are the seven "gifts" of the Holy Spirit. The seven Gifts of the Holy Spirit are: Wisdom, Understanding, Knowledge, Counsel, Piety, Fortitude and Fear of the Lord.

The world needs the Fruits and Gifts of the Holy Spirit to find and promote peace. (Article 66 from my book: God is Love.)

121
Coming out of Covid19 Restrictions

I have received full vaccination against Covid19. After doing so, at first I was very exuberant, for I could now visit face to face persons near and dear to me or even meet new people instead of suffering from all that social isolation. I had such a feeling of "freedom". Covid19 restrictions brought me to realize what is important in life especially personal contact with others.

I am thankful to God for inspiring the researchers to provide a vaccine so rapidly against the virus. Also, I thank those responsible for administering the vaccine. My local experience with that was very good.

I believe most of us are coming of out of the "scourge" of Covid19 much stronger as Job did in the Old Testament after his faith was tested by personal disasters. I am looking forward to more contact with family and close friends and celebrating the new freedom which comes from God, for God is Happiness.

122
Is Love Proper?

Love is Proper. Too many people believe being proper is distinct from being loving. To them, being proper means to follow the "formal" rules of society. I do believe that if breaking such a rule is "rude" or damaging in any way, then we should not break the rule.

However, if following the formal rule, rules out Love, it is not proper to follow it. The right thing to do is Love; therefore Love is Proper, and it comes from God, our source of Happiness.

123 Freedom: Is it a Myth?

I have said that we are bound by laws, both societal (man-made) and physical (gravity). Finally, we are bound by God's Laws. All these laws can and do inhibit our freedom, but do not deny it completely.

In conclusion, Happiness can be attained, like Freedom, but not completely in the lifetime. Both can be attained on a continuum of relativity, so not absolutely. Finally, it is possible to be very Happy, even with very little Freedom. Happiness is not completely dependent on Freedom, but on our Love of God and Others.

124 Is There a Difference between Fun and Good Times?

Fun is an escape from serious deliberation often manifested by laughter and upbeat exuberance or elation. Good times, on the other hand, occurs when we are living in a period of enjoying contentment, possibly, as a reward or result of doing good deeds.

Fun is more temporary, I believe, than good times, which are actually periods of Happiness.

Do not assume that good times will end, but graciously leave fun behind to do serious deliberation when necessary to bring us true Happiness, which comes from LOVING GOD and OTHERS. God is Happiness!

125
Is Money the Root of All Evil?

In high school, a classmate said to me: "Money is the root of all evil." She must have based the statement on a reading from the Old Testament. However, that reading is NOT that "Money is the root of all evil", but that the "Love of Money" is the root of all evil. *NO – IT SAYS "MUCH"*

Jesus said that we cannot serve both money and God. We must choose. Money is meant to serve us, not for us to serve money. It can serve us in many ways in which it can satisfy real needs or legitimate desires for which we spend the money. Or it can be given to others to benefit them. But, money has no value "in itself" and should NOT be served as if it were a "religion" with rules to follow for simply accumulating money for the Love of Money. We must serve God to find true Happiness, for money alone will not give us that reward.

126
Fairness in Relationships

It has been said it is better to Give than to Receive. I have said that we should not expect reciprocation from others when giving our love to them, whether it be in thought, word or deed. (Article 64, God is Love). God always rewards us for giving love to Him and to others. But, at times, we do consider FAIRNESS in a relationship. It is human to do so. If we do not receive reciprocation in a relationship, we must consider our own needs. We do not have to "hang on a lover's cross" for others or be a martyr for them. God does not expect that.

Our patience is NOT unlimited and we have the right to end a relationship, if it is not fair. It is up to us, based on Prayer with God, to decide how long we can keep on GIVING with little Receiving of Love. If the other person is incapable of returning love in a robust fashion (elderly, children or disabled) then we should not terminate our gift of communication with that person. However, if the person is capable of reciprocating a gift of Love to us , but decides not to do so, I believe we are free to terminate that relationship if we are not bound by legal concerns (children of families, for example). If others do not reciprocate our gift of love, we must remember that GOD STILL LOVES US AND THANKS US FOR OUR EFFORTS.

127
Co-operation vs. Competition

Life should involve more teamwork or co-operation than competition. We should all try to work together to build the "Family of Man". Songs have been written to unify Mankind through its music. Such songs should, I believe, be taken seriously rather than just another 'hum drum" song.

If we look around each day, we often can find someplace where there is a need for Love. Loving God and others is the greatest contribution we can give to God and Others. This does not mean just sharing "sex" between lovers, but wanting to do the best for others and not just for ourselves. It is everyone's responsibility to do so. It requires more co-operation, which can bring us together, rather than just competition, which is OK at times, but can tear us apart.

128
Trust in God and Others Can Bring Us Happiness

I find it easy to trust God. However, trusting people is difficult for me at times. I believe others agree with that view. If we have a solid relationship with God, we trust Him. But to find a solid relationship with others, particularly those that we do not know very well is more difficult, but that does not mean that we should "give up" on the relationship if we know that the other person is reasonably trying to reciprocate our "giving " to them.

Trusting GOD and OTHERS can bring us Happiness, but sometimes we must take a "leap of faith" to find that trust. If we deem it is worth it to do so, we should do it to find Happiness for us and for them.

129
Is the "Devil" Responsible for Our Sins"

"Satan" or the "Devil" was and still is a concept denoting an "evil spirit" trying to tempt mankind into doing "evil" or sinning against God and, I believe, against Mankind. So it is "tempting" for us to blame the "devil" when we commit sinful acts in thoughts, word or deeds.

Sinful "thoughts" can be considered "temptation" and we should not "entertain" them, but dismiss them as evil. Likewise for sinful words or deeds; they are evil and, of course, should not be done. The saying goes, "What do we say when Satan tempts us? Be gone, Satan!"

Morality still matters, of course. But to blame the devil for our sins is simply making an excuse for them rather than admitting guilt and asking God for forgiveness. Sin is our own fault, so do not blame the "devil". By repenting of our sins, we can be reconciled to God, despite the "devil". Then we can find true Happiness, for God is Love and God is Happiness!

130
The Mandate to Love

Jesus Christ gave a mandate to mankind: Love God with all you heart, mind, soul and strength, and Love your neighbor as yourself. (Neighbor, I believe, is meant to "include" everyone") If we do not follow this mandate, our lives will be "short" on Happiness. If we do not Love One Another, it shows that we do not really Love God. Scripture says 'if one says he loves God, but hates his brother, he is a liar." The Mandate to Love must be followed to find Peace and Happiness with God and Others.

131
Love: Does it Mean that We Never have to Say: I am Sorry?

NO! All of us make mistakes sometimes and have misunderstandings with others. However, there it's a way to get out of this situation: Simply say "I am sorry and ask for forgiveness". I have done this sometimes in my marriage. Humility is necessary to say: "I am sorry", after INNOCENTLY offending someone. We may not feel we owe the other an apology, because we did not intentionally do anything to offend the other. But, as in my wife's case, she was offended, so I swallowed my pride and apologized to her to keep the relationship intact. It was over something so simple as telling her that I could not answer her question about the music vans for the band, when I was turning off the road into the parking lot to find a place to park at the theatre of the Oak Ridge Boys, which I was doing for the first time ever. I was under too much stress to answer her question at the time. So she was offended by what she considered rudely ignoring her. However, after I apologized, she forgave me and we moved forward.

I apologized, not because I thought I was wrong, but because I wanted to save our marriage. We have to pick our battles. If it is over something trivial, we have lost perspective on what's is really important. To me, what was important was my marriage.

132
Is it Better to Give than Receive?

Yes, it is. We can experience the Joy of inner peace when we give with "no strings attached." Doing so prevents us from falling into the trappings of receiving material goods for our gift. I view the "gifts" of my books this way: no trappings to tarnish the gift with material things such as money. I am not suggesting that receiving monetary gifts is wrong. Until now it has not been my way for my books. It gives me freedom to know there were no strings attached. It is truly better to give than receive, if we can do it. God gives us the reward—Happiness!

133
The Gift of Love

It is truly a gift to give Love to somebody hoping that we will receive love back—a real bonus! For me, my power to give comes from the Holy Spirit, the third person in the Blessed Trinity who inspires me through the Power of Love. His power is a gift to me and inspires me to write and I am grateful for it. The writings have given me much Happiness which I have tried to share with others in my books. God is Happiness!

134
Could the Legacy of Jesus be Everlasting Life by Following His Two Commandments?

Yes. I believe that it is. The most important statement Jesus ever made was regarding "offering everlasting life" but only if we followed his Commandments of Love of God and our Neighbor as Ourselves. The everlasting life He offered was, in my opinion, everlasting Happiness!

135
Today: Opportunity for Happiness

The world today has more opportunity for Happiness than ever before. Technology has brought us so far towards making our lives connected and even entertained. Furthermore, advances in medicine have made it possible to reduce the dangers of Covid19 and other diseases. Even manual laborer has been reduced.

The only thing threatening and even preventing Happiness for us is the lack of trust brought on by "scams" using the technology to swindle people out of their money, and the fear brought on by criminals which endanger our peace with violence and disrespect of both our bodies and our properties.

However, let us not lose hope for all the good that has been accomplished especially through workers in all walks of life. "Hats off" to scientists and engineers, medical persons, military, religious, business persons, service personnel and persons in all walks of life.

Let us move forward towards Love and Understanding and, yes, COMPROMISE—EVEN IN GOVERNMENT to build a better tomorrow for HAPPINESS FOR EVERYONE.

Finally, some people believe that they simply go to the cemetery in a casket after they die. WAKE UP! JESUS CHRIST offered and still offers EVERLASTING LIFE to those that believe in Him. if you accept this, your soul will not go to the grave, but to Heaven, I believe, immediately after you die. You do not have to wait for the Resurrection of the Body at the end of the World when Jesus may have His Second Coming.

Jesus said to the thief on the Cross when He was crucified; "This day you will be with me in Paradise." Thus, there was no grave for the thief's soul, because He saw that Jesus was good and believed in Him. CHEER UP! EVERLASTING HAPPINESS AWAITS THOSE WHO DIE IN BODY, BUT BELIEVE IN GOD AND STAY IN HIS GOOD GRACES. I BELIEVE THAT IS THE PROMISE OF JESUS CHRIST.

GOD IS HAPPINESS! GOD BLESS ALL OF YOU!

Michael John DeNucci lives in Cumberland, WI and is a freelance writer for God and Mankind.

Michael DeNucci attended his first two years of high school at Holy Cross Seminary in Lacrosse, Wisconsin and then returned to graduate from Cumberland High School. He went on to earn his Bachelor's Degree in Political Science from the College of St. Thomas, St. Paul, Minnesota, attended the University of Wisconsin at Madison partially completing an MBA, and earning a Master's Degree in Industrial Relations from the University of Minnesota. He is an Army Veteran who has served stateside and in Germany. He has held a variety of jobs over his lifetime which have broadened his perspectives on the relationship of God and Mankind.

Other Books by Michael John DeNucci

"Thoughts and Writings"
"Fishing for Heaven"
"God is Love"
"Is Love the Truth?"
"Is God Freedom?"
"God Is the Truth"
"Is Love Freedom?"
"Is God Mercy?"
"Is God Peace?"
"Happiness is the Truth"
"God is Justice"